CONTENTS

INTRODUCTION

Alma McGowen was a new girl at school when she enrolled in the Spencer County School District in Louisville, Kentucky. It was 1992, and she was in sixth grade. From the second day, things started to go wrong for Alma. A first grader shouted that she was "that German gay girl." Alma complained to the school counselor, who talked to students about the importance of acceptance. But the harassment continued. A high school student on the school bus used sexually explicit language when talking to Alma. She complained again, and the boy was kicked off the bus for a few days. When he returned, he continued to target Alma.

Over the next couple of years, the harassment grew worse. Students taunted Alma or touched her inappropriately in almost every class. Once, a group of boys surrounded her and started to tear at her clothes. One of the boys began to take his pants off, saying that he was going to have sex with her. Alma complained numerous times to school officials, teachers, and youth advocates. Even when they spoke to her tormenters, the harassment only grew worse afterwards.

In 1995, Alma filed a formal complaint stating that the sexual harassment violated her right to receive education opportunities. She was diagnosed with depression, and she eventually withdrew from school. In 1998, Alma's case went to trial. A jury ruled in her favor and awarded her $220,000. An appeals court confirmed the verdict, finding that the sexual harassment had been severe and pervasive, that the school district had been aware of the harassment, and that it had shown "deliberate indifference" to the circumstances.

THE LAW PERSONAL HEALTH
YOUR LEGAL RIGHTS

JASON PORTERFIELD

ROSEN
PUBLISHING

New York

Published in 2016 by The Rosen Publishing Group, Inc.
29 East 21st Street, New York, NY 10010

Expert Reviewer: Lindsay A. Lewis, Esq.

Library of Congress Cataloging-in-Publication Data

Porterfield, Jason, author.
The law and personal health : your legal rights/Jason Porterfield.
    pages cm.—(Know your rights)
Includes bibliographical references and index.
ISBN 978-1-4777-8052-7 (library bound)—
ISBN 978-1-4777-8614-7 (pbk.)—
ISBN 978-1-4777-8615-4 (6-pack)
1. Public health laws—United States—Juvenile literature. 2. Informed consent (Medical law)—United States—Juvenile literature. 3. Confidential communications—Physicians—United States—Juvenile literature. I. Title.
KF3775.P67 2016
344.7303'21—dc23

A student experiencing harassment may feel isolated and helpless, but there are recourses for a teen in such a situation. Schools have a responsibility to provide a safe learning environment.

Harassment is a civil rights issue since it can affect people's access to certain privileges regardless of factors such as sex or race. But it is also a health issue when people who experience harassment become depressed or experience other psychological and physical health consequences. High-profile cases such as Alma's have led to many schools adopting inclusive policies that combat harassment. Alma knew her rights concerning harassment, and the courts backed her up.

As a teenager, you have certain rights concerning a broad range of personal health issues. But, as a minor, you're still required to have the consent of a parent or guardian for most medical decisions. There are some exceptions. These concern issues that teens may prefer to keep private, such as reproductive health care, substance abuse counseling, and mental health treatment. When you're facing a health issue for which you'd prefer to receive confidential treatment, it might seem like you have no place to turn for help. If you're aware of your legal rights concerning your health, the knowledge can make a daunting situation seem much more manageable.

CHAPTER 1

CONSENT, CONFIDENTIALITY, AND PRIVACY

As a young adult, you may be beginning to make your own health care decisions for the first time. It's important that you start out by establishing good habits in caring for your well-being. If you have a concern about a health issue, you should see a doctor or other medical professional.

But many teenagers are reluctant to take their problems to a doctor, and one of the main reasons is a concern about confidentiality. What if friends at school found out about an embarrassing medical condition? Or employers or parents? Teens may be unwilling to seek help for issues such as sexually transmitted diseases, depression, or substance abuse if it meant that others might find out. Yet all of these are urgent health matters that should be addressed by a medical professional.

Patient confidentiality forbids medical service providers from sharing personal health information without the patient's consent. But the law only fully applies to adults—people age eighteen or older. For a minor, parents are responsible for making most medical decisions and have the right to access most medical information.

Health care providers are required by law to keep patient information confidential, both in a health care setting and in dealing with patient records.

MAKING DECISIONS ABOUT YOUR HEALTH

Before a patient receives medical care, he or she must give consent for the treatment or process. By giving consent, the patient indicates that he or she understands the information about the treatment and authorizes the doctor to administer medical care. For serious procedures, a patient must give written informed consent. During the informed consent process, health care providers provide a full explanation of the treatment and risks. The patient asks questions and weighs options before signing the consent form.

A patient must have the capacity to understand the information in order to grant consent. If an individual is not competent to make decisions concerning medical care, another adult will make the decisions on his or her behalf. For example, parents make the medical decisions for young children. In general, minors, those under the age of eighteen, must have parental consent in order to receive health care services.

As a teenager, you must have a parent or guardian's consent for most medical treatments. In general, both biological and adoptive parents have full right to consent to medical treatment for their children. In some situations, however, the issue of granting legal consent can be complicated. Some parents or guardians may not have the right to grant medical consent for their children. These include divorced parents without legal custody, stepparents who have not adopted their stepchildren, and foster parents. The matter of medical consent is even more complex for minors involved in the juvenile justice system. In such cases, medical consent may be granted by a social worker, a probation officer, a juvenile court official, or a representative of certain other social service agencies. Specific laws concerning consent vary from state to state.

Under some circumstances, teenagers may be granted consent rights. Legally emancipated minors can give consent. So can teenagers who are married or serving in the armed forces. Minors who are parents have the right

Health care workers take careful measures to protect patient records from unauthorized access—physical records are kept locked up, and access to electronic records is restricted.

to grant consent for their children, and in some states, they can make medical decisions for themselves as well.

Minors do have the right to consent to certain types of health services. These include reproductive care, treatment of certain diseases (such as sexually transmitted diseases and contagious diseases), mental health services, and substance abuse treatment. A minor can also receive treatment without consent in an emergency situation.

UNDERSTANDING CONFIDENTIALITY

Confidentiality is an important aspect of a doctor's relationship with a patient. Patient confidentiality requires that a doctor keep a patient's medical information private. Access is restricted to health care providers and other agencies involved in health care operations, such as insurance companies. A doctor cannot disclose a patient's medical information to family, friends, or employers without the patient's consent. If a patient is in the hospital and a friend or family member asks the doctor about the patient's condition, the doctor's response must be, "Ask the patient," unless he or she has received permission to share information. Health care workers who handle electronic medical records must take care to keep them secure from unauthorized access.

The assurance of confidentiality fosters a trusting relationship between patient and doctor. A patient is less likely to share highly personal details about health conditions if he or she does not believe that the doctor will keep the details confidential. In order to determine an appropriate course of treatment, the doctor must possess as much information as possible about the patient's condition.

The issue of confidentiality can become more complex when the patient is an adolescent. Under the law, parents have the right to grant medical consent for their teenage son or daughter. Minors are not considered to have the capacity to make their own medical decisions. As a result, adolescents don't have complete confidentiality with their doctors—their medical information must be shared with their parents. Sometimes, this situation can lead to conflict over the teen's

It's important that adolescents share their health concerns with their health care providers, but concerns about privacy may make some teens unwilling to talk freely.

desire for privacy. During adolescence, teenagers begin asserting their independence as they make the transition to adulthood. They may resent having their parents knowing their most personal medical details.

Most hospitals and other health care providers have policies for dealing with the issue of confidentiality when treating adolescents. A doctor may discuss confidentiality independently with the patient and the parents. He or she may encourage the parents to listen to and address their teenager's concerns about treatment. The doctor may emphasize to the patient that everyone involved in the treat-

ment process has only the patient's interests in mind. The end goal is to create an environment of trust and open communication in making health care decisions.

Adolescence is also a time when teenagers begin testing boundaries. Teenagers are notorious for taking risks without considering the possible consequences—some research has shown that the adolescent brain is not yet capable of mature judgment and decision making. Some teens become sexually active or experiment with drugs and alcohol.

Teenagers are often unwilling—either out of embarrassment or fear of getting into trouble—to discuss matters related to their personal health with their parents, especially regarding conditions linked to risky behaviors. Examples include sexually transmitted diseases and reproductive health issues, including pregnancy. In addition, many mental health conditions emerge during adolescence. Many teens don't feel comfortable admitting to mental health concerns such as depression, eating disorders, or suicidal thoughts to their parents. If left untreated, teens' medical conditions can have lifelong consequences. And in many cases, teens do not possess adequate knowledge or resources to deal with these health issues on their own.

Over the last few decades, lawmakers have acknowledged the importance of allowing teenagers to access some types of health services without requiring parental consent or notification. Doctors can generally promise confidentiality in treating issues related to reproductive health, mental health, and substance abuse, although laws vary from state to state. Some states explicitly grant minors the ability to give legal consent for services such as contraception, while others have no relevant laws or have laws that are subject to restrictions. These restrictions may include age requirements or limits on types of treatment. Some states allow a doctor to use his or her discretion in deciding whether to notify a parent.

PRIVACY AND YOUR HEALTH

A teenager seeking a confidential consultation concerning sensitive personal health issues or questions might be tempted to cry out, "What do I do now?" The first step is to check up on your rights to medical confidentiality according to the laws in your state. According to federal law, when a teenager can legally consent to medical treatment, he or she is granted the same legal confidentiality as an adult.

But adolescents can only consent to a small range of medical services, and these vary from state to state. Your state government website will provide a description of relevant minor consent laws.

In addition, doctors are sometimes unsure themselves about minors' rights to consent and confidentiality. Every hospital and health care provider should have policies and procedures for addressing confidentiality issues concerning a minor's treatment. In practice, however, doctors are sometimes uncertain about circumstances in which a minor patient can legally grant consent. Before you discuss your specific health issues with a doctor or health care provider, ask about patient confidentiality for minors and make sure that you understand your rights and restrictions.

Another obstacle to teenagers receiving confidential medical care is the matter of payment. A teen's insurance plan may pay for the costs, but most teens are covered by family insurance plans. Medical offices attempt to preserve confidentiality in billing, but some insurance companies won't pay for treatment without being informed in full detail about the medical services that were provided. If you file an insurance claim, the itemized bill received by your parents may reveal specific medical services and lab tests. Alternatively, you could pay for services on your own. In some states, adolescents may be able to access low-cost treatments or reimbursement programs for certain health services.

There are certain circumstances in which doctors are required by law to break confidentiality. These occur

LAWS PROTECTING YOUR PRIVACY

Concerns about the privacy of one's sensitive health information go beyond a fear of embarrassment. A breach of privacy can lead to discrimination, fraud, and misuse of data. As electronic records and other high-tech innovations make health records easier to access and share, laws have been updated to protect patients' confidentiality. The Health Insurance Portability and Accountability Act (HIPAA) of 1996 includes a rule that restricts the disclosure of health information by health care providers. The HIPAA Privacy Rule establishes guidelines for handling health information and establishes certain rights for patients concerning their records. HIPAA does not expand minors' consent rights, but it does grant minors many of the same protections as adults for instances in which they do have the right to consent.

In some cases, it may be necessary or beneficial for a patient to authorize a HIPAA release that allows health care providers to provide personal health information to others. Attorneys, for instance, will often seek releases from their clients so that they can effectively litigate medical, mental health, and substance abuse issues related to their clients' cases. The standard HIPAA release form thus covers not only medical records, history, and treatment, but also contains separate releases for HIV information, mental health records and information, and drug and alcohol treatment information, where applicable.

The private information of minors is also protected by the Family Educational Rights and Privacy Act (FERPA), which addresses the privacy of educational records, including some records related to health. In general, a parent must consent for the release of any records covered by FERPA. Once a student turns eighteen, the rights to the information are transferred to the student.

Teens may choose to pay their own bills to avoid having certain health care services listed on their parents' insurance statements, but for many teens, this option is not affordable.

mostly in situations in which it is necessary to protect the minor's safety or preserve public health. By law, doctors must report cases of abuse or neglect to social service agencies. They may be required to notify the authorities if a patient represents a threat to himself or herself or to others. Doctors must also report cases of certain contagious diseases to the health department.

17

CHAPTER 2

REPRODUCTIVE HEALTH

Sex education and teenage reproductive health are controversial topics. Debate over sex education curricula and programs often involves discussions of morality and religion. Some adults believe that people should wait until marriage to have sex, and that allowing adolescents access to contraception and reproductive health care encourages teen sexual activity. But many health care workers and policy makers believe that education and confidential health care provide teens with information and resources that can help them make intelligent decisions about their sexual health. They emphasize the importance of confidentiality in reproductive health matters since many teens are unwilling to seek care if they have to notify their parents.

Data about teens' sexual activity highlight their need for access to health care services. According to a 2011 survey by the Centers for Disease Control and Prevention (CDC), nearly half of all high school students are sexually active. Adolescents are more likely to acquire sexually transmitted diseases (STDs) than adults. Teenage girls are more likely to have unplanned pregnancies.

Many health care organizations and social service agencies offer information and resources related to teen sexual health. The American Medical Association (AMA) endorses comprehensive sex education programs, and the American

Most states require that students receive sex education in public schools, but specific curriculum policies and guidelines vary greatly from one state to another.

Academy of Pediatrics (AAP) provides information about teen sexuality for parents and adolescents on their website, healthychildren.com. The U.S. Department of Health and Human Services (HHS) offers resources related to reproductive health through its Office of Adolescent Health, and the online service MedLinePlus provides a wealth of information, news, and statistics in its Teen Sexual Health section.

A federal program called Title X provides access to family planning resources and other preventative health services. The program funds family planning clinics across the country—about 4,400 clinics in nearly three-quarters of counties in the United States. Title X was established in 1970 to provide affordable services to low-income individuals, including teens. Health care services provided through Title X are required by law to be confidential, although health care providers may encourage teens to discuss their medical issues with their parents.

CONTRACEPTIVE SERVICES

Contraceptives provide a means of preventing pregnancy. Some contraceptives also prevent the transmission of STDs. Condoms are generally the most accessible type of contraception—anyone can buy them at drugstores. Some schools have programs that distribute condoms to students, but these are not widespread.

Family planning clinics offer a wide variety of birth control methods, most of which require a prescription. When a teenager visits a clinic, a health care provider will take a brief health history, discuss various options, and help her decide which birth control is the best for her circumstances.

Volunteers distribute free condoms during an HIV testing event. Condoms are widely available and help prevent pregnancies as well as the spread of STDs, including HIV.

Many clinics will provide hormonal contraception without requiring a physical exam, though they may require a urine sample for a pregnancy test. The teenager may be able to "quick start" a contraceptive method on the day of the visit, although the specific process varies depending on the method. It may be as simple as receiving a single shot that is effective for three months or picking up a supply of birth control pills. Other methods—such as a diaphragm—may require fitting; an intrauterine device (IUD) and implants must be inserted by a trained medical provider.

Teens' rights to confidentiality in obtaining contraceptive services vary from state to state. A 1977 Supreme Court case found that teens have the same right to privacy as adults in making decisions about reproductive health, and no state altogether denies consent for teens seeking contraception. In some states, minors over the age of twelve can legally consent to contraceptive services. In other states, the minimum age is fourteen. Some states impose additional conditions, such as allowing doctors to notify parents or restricting access to certain categories of minors, such as teens who are married. Regardless of state law, clinics federally funded by Title X can provide confidential care.

Another service for women provided by clinics is emergency contraception, also referred to as the morning-after pill or by its brand name, Plan B. Emergency contraception prevents pregnancy when taken up to five days after unprotected sex. The most common form is a single pill. In 2013, the Food and Drug Administration (FDA) approved the sale of Plan B One-Step to people of any age without the need for a prescription. Generic forms of this drug are also available to minors without a prescription.

PRENATAL CARE

The United States has a high rate of teen pregnancies compared to other developed countries, and most teen pregnancies are unplanned. Most sex education classes and family planning programs emphasize pregnancy prevention. But if a teenage girl does become pregnant, it is important for her own health and that of the child that she seek prenatal care, which is the health care a woman receives

Whether a positive pregnancy test is welcome news or not, it means that a young woman should make a fresh commitment to taking charge of her personal health.

during pregnancy. Teenagers are at risk for certain complications during pregnancy. The baby may be more likely to be born prematurely or have a low birth weight.

The first step is confirming a pregnancy. Home pregnancy tests are available at drugstores. Clinics can also administer pregnancy tests. If the test is positive, the teen should make an appointment with a doctor. Health care providers monitor the health of the mother and baby, track the baby's growth, and treat any possible complications. They will also explain what to expect during a pregnancy and offer healthy lifestyle tips.

Teens generally have the right to confidential prenatal care. A few states require that minors be a certain age in order to consent. Fourteen states allow a doctor to notify the teen's parents if he or she believes that it's in the teen's best interests, but notification is not a legal requirement.

Motherhood is an immense responsibility, and a pregnant teenager may decide that she is not ready to raise a child. One possible option in this case is to give the child up for adoption. Most states allow minors to legally put their child up for adoption without the knowledge or consent of their parents or other adults. Some states require that the teen mother be represented by legal counsel during the adoption process, and several other states require either consent or notification of the teen mother's parents.

A pregnant teenager who does not wish to give birth may consider getting an abortion. Most states require parental consent, parental notification, or a court order for minors seeking abortions. Even emancipated minors may be prohibited from consenting to an abortion. Federally funded Title X programs do not provide abortions. If a parent refuses consent, a minor may be able to petition the court to grant consent.

STD TESTING AND TREATMENT

According to the CDC, young adults are at a higher risk of contracting STDs than the general population. People between the ages of fifteen and twenty-four make up well over half of all new cases of sexually transmitted diseases. Untreated STDs can cause long-term health problems. Young adults who are sexually active should be tested

THE AFFORDABLE CARE ACT

In 2010, the Affordable Care Act (ACA), sometimes known as Obamacare, was signed into law. The law represented the biggest overhaul of the country's health care system in decades. One of the act's main goals was to extend insurance coverage to nearly all Americans. It also aimed to reduce overall health care costs. Measures in the bill affected consumers, insurers, and health care providers. Enactment of the provisions was gradually phased in over a matter of years after the bill's passage, although legal and logistical challenges caused delays.

The law includes several provisions that benefit teens and young adults. It allows young adults to stay on their parents' health plan until age twenty-six. It also provides free contraceptive care and preventative services, including HIV screening. Another provision of the law established the Personal Responsibility Education Program (PREP), which awards grants to states for the purpose of developing innovative strategies for preventing pregnancy and STDs as well as helping teens develop skills that will prepare them for adulthood.

regularly for STDs, including HIV, for the sake of their own health and also to prevent the possibility of transmitting diseases to their partners. Many young adults with HIV, the virus that causes AIDS, were infected through sexual contact. According to the Department of Health and Human Services, about one in five people with HIV are unaware that they are carrying the virus.

STD testing may involve a physical exam as well as analysis of blood or urine samples. Treatment varies

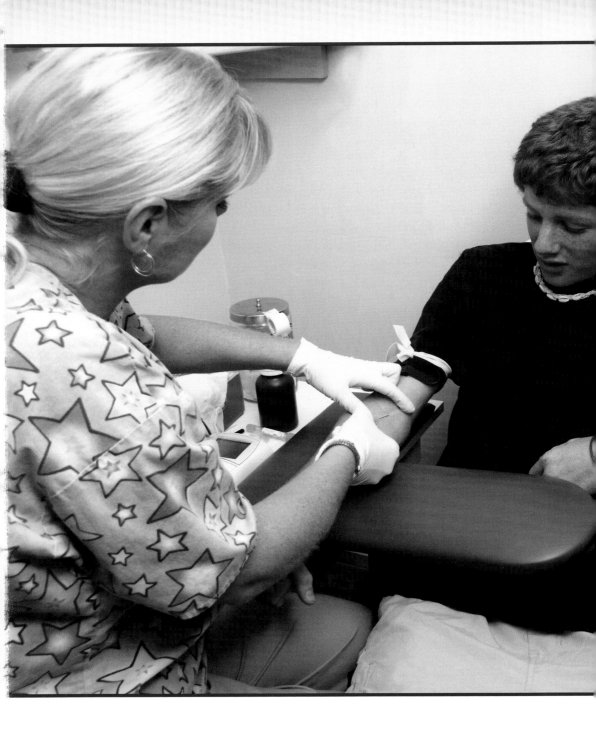

depending on the particular disease. Some STDs can be cured with a round of antibiotics. Others are incurable, but the symptoms can be managed with medications. HIV/AIDS requires lifelong treatment.

Minors are allowed to consent to STD and HIV testing and treatment in all states, with some restrictions. Some states require a minimum age, usually twelve or fourteen. Some states allow doctors to notify the parents if they believe it's in the minor's best interests. (One exception is Iowa, which requires that parents be notified of a positive HIV test.) Some states do not allow minors to consent to HIV treatment. Regardless of state law, clinics federally funded by Title X can provide confidential STD and HIV testing.

A minor with an STD is likely to want to conceal the fact from friends and family, but a health care provider may encourage a teen with an STD to disclose the fact to his or her partner. Past or current partners may have been infected and require treatment. Some teen health websites offer tips on how to start an open conversation about STDs. The law may even require disclosure—in some states, someone who transmits HIV to a partner without disclosure can be prosecuted.

Many clinics take measures to make teens comfortable when getting tested or discussing health problems. Examination rooms are private and secure, and patients are given a chance to ask questions about their concerns.

CHAPTER 3

MENTAL HEALTH

Adolescence is a critical period in the development of the brain, which undergoes a major reorganization process during the teen years. Teenagers have a greater capacity for learning than adults, but they are also more likely to take risks. Since teens process information differently from adults, they may be more likely to make decisions based on emotions without weighing consequences. Hormonal changes also affect behavior.

Many mental health disorders tend to manifest during adolescence. According to the National Institute of Mental Health, about 20 percent of teens are seriously affected by a mental disorder at some point during their lives. Mental illness can damage relationships with family and friends and affect performance at school and work. The consequences can even be tragic—according to the CDC, suicide is the third-leading cause of death among people between the ages of fourteen and twenty-two.

Treatment of mental health disorders among adolescents can be crucial to preventing relapses in adulthood. For example, effective therapy can reduce the chances that a teenager suffering from depression would develop chronic depression as an adult. Nonetheless, only about half of all adolescents experiencing mental health disorders receive treatment. Some teenagers do not have access to mental health services. In addition, for many people,

Adolescence is a turbulent phase of life for many teens, but extreme changes in feelings or behaviors could be symptoms of mental illness.

mental illness still bears a stigma. Adolescents may fail to seek help because they feel ashamed for suffering from a mental health disorder.

GETTING MENTAL HEALTH TREATMENT

Confidentiality and trust can be very important to teens seeking mental health services. A teen experiencing mental health issues such as depression or anxiety may not want a therapist or other mental health professional sharing personal details with parents, especially since he or she might be discussing family issues. Teenagers might even prefer to seek treatment without offering any explanation to their parents, whether due to embarrassment or fear of disapproval.

As with most teen confidentiality and consent issues, the law varies from state to state. Fewer than half of all states explicitly allow minors to consent to certain mental health services. Many states impose restrictions, such as a minimum age for consent. States may also grant mental health professionals discretion in determining whether the teenager has the maturity to make informed decisions concerning care. In many cases, if the mental health professional believes that the teen may pose a threat to his or her own well-being or the well-being of others, he or she may notify parents. Even when a mental health provider does involve parents, however, he or she may choose not to disclose certain information if it would be damaging to the treatment process.

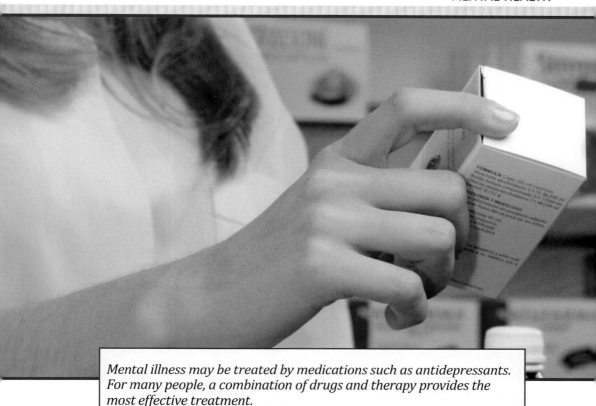

Mental illness may be treated by medications such as antidepressants. For many people, a combination of drugs and therapy provides the most effective treatment.

Treatment for mental health disorders can be outpatient or inpatient. Teens who seek outpatient therapy continue with their daily lives while undergoing treatment. Many types of health care providers offer mental health services. These include mental health specialists—such as psychiatrists (who are medical doctors), psychologists, and social workers—who may work at psychiatry departments of hospitals, mental health clinics, social service agencies, or school-based health centers. The process generally begins with an evaluation, after which the mental health professional makes a diagnosis and recommends a treatment plan. The treatment may include medications as well as therapy.

INVOLUNTARY COMMITMENT

An individual suffering from serious mental illness may refuse to admit that he or she needs help. In some cases, especially when the person poses a threat to self or others, he or she may be committed involuntarily to inpatient treatment at a psychiatric facility. For adults, this process generally requires a court order. For children and adolescents, however, parents have the right to consent to medical treatment for them.

This does not mean that parents have the legal right to have a child committed without medical justification. Mental health professionals must recommend that the child be admitted for treatment, and they will do so only if it is in the patient's best interests. Laws concerning involuntary commitment of minors vary from state to state. Minors over a certain age may have the legal right to file an objection to the admission. Mental health providers generally have the discretion not to disclose details discussed during therapy to the parents.

Parents sometimes have great difficulty finding effective treatment for a child with a severe mental health disorder. They may have trouble with insurance, availability of appropriate programs, or legal barriers. In some cases, desperate parents may relinquish custody of a child in order to qualify for state mental health services.

There are many different types of therapy, such as individual therapy, cognitive behavioral therapy, group therapy, family therapy, or behavior management techniques. In some states, parents must consent to certain services, such as medication. Other conditions may also apply, such as a limitation on length of treatment.

Inpatient treatment involves admission to a hospital or other mental health facility. Inpatient care is more intensive than outpatient treatment, and patients admitted usually have significant mental health issues. Some states allow minors to consent to inpatient treatment, although some level of parental notification or involvement is usually required. In Pennsylvania, for example, a minor can consent to inpatient treatment, and a parent must be notified. The parent cannot override the minor's consent. If the teen decides to revoke consent, however, the parent may opt to continue treatment against the teen's wishes if recommended by a doctor.

MENTAL HEALTH AND THE JUVENILE JUSTICE SYSTEM

Mental illness increases the likelihood that an adolescent will be brought to the attention of the juvenile court. According to the National Alliance on Mental Illness, about 70 percent of adolescents involved in the juvenile justice system have at least one mental illness. These teens are more likely than others to have a serious mental illness, and the suicide rate is much higher among young offenders than average. Mental health issues can affect a juvenile's competency, or his or her ability to understand and participate in legal proceedings.

The juvenile justice system aims to rehabilitate rather than merely punish young offenders. Some states have instituted mental health courts that focus on treating teens with an underlying mental illness that contributes to their delinquent behavior. There is no national juvenile justice system, and specific laws and policies vary greatly from one state to another.

Over half of adolescents who are found guilty of juvenile offenses are given a sentence of probation, often

In the right facility, teens in the juvenile-justice system might have access to mental health treatment and other resources that can be crucial to rehabilitation.

accompanied by requirements such as performing community service or paying a fine. In some cases, a juvenile's disposition, or sentence, may include mental health services such as counseling, anger management classes, or family therapy.

Juvenile offenders who are sent to correctional facilities may also receive treatment for mental health disorders. Types of correctional facilities vary widely—they include residential facilities, "boot camp" programs, group homes, and many more—and many offer mental health services such as therapy, counseling, and medication. Young offenders are generally screened for mental illnesses and suicide risk upon arrival. For some adolescents, the trauma of being separated from family and thrust into an unfamiliar, hostile environment may increase the risk of suicide attempts.

Although policy makers recognize the benefits of mental health care for adolescents in the juvenile justice system, young offenders often fail to receive adequate mental health care. Many teen offenders aren't properly screened for mental health problems unless they are sent to a correctional facility. Even then, many facilities are overcrowded and lack the resources to provide comprehensive services to young offenders with mental health needs. These same issues can follow teens into the adult criminal justice system where, in certain circumstances, those under eighteen can wind up.

CHAPTER 4

SUBSTANCE ABUSE

In 2002, the Supreme Court heard a case regarding drug testing for high school students. An Oklahoma school district implemented a policy requiring all students involved in extracurricular activities to consent to drug testing even when there were no grounds for suspicion of drug use. Two students and their parents challenged the policy, arguing that it violated their Fourth Amendment rights concerning unreasonable search and seizure.

The Court ruled that the drug testing was constitutional. It concluded that the school district had an important interest in preventing drug abuse and that students participating in extracurricular activities had a diminished expectation of privacy. The ruling expanded on a previous ruling that permitted drug testing of athletes. A dissenting opinion raised the objection that students involved in extracurricular activities were actually less likely than average to be at risk for drug abuse. It also affirmed a lower court's ruling that random drug testing was unwarranted unless it was responding to an identifiable drug abuse problem among the students.

The case illustrates the complexity in finding a balance between students' right to privacy and the school's interest in deterring drug use, identifying students with substance abuse issues, and maintaining a secure learning environment. Similar justifications are used in implementing workplace drug testing. In addition, the law can intervene further if an adolescent who commits a crime has a drug problem. Studies have shown that alcohol and drug abuse are often the underlying cause of criminal activity, both among minors and adults. It is in society's best interests to address drug abuse among young offenders, even if the underlying offense did not involve drugs or alcohol.

DRUG TESTING AND YOUR RIGHTS

In most states, the law permits schools to test students for drugs such as marijuana, cocaine, opioids, amphetamines, and PCP.

Under some circumstances, adolescents may be required to undergo drug testing at school, at work, in a hospital, or even at home or due to a court order. The process generally requires a urine sample, which is analyzed in a lab for illicit substances. A test may be conducted as a routine precaution or as a result of reasonable suspicion of drug use.

Schools can legally require drug tests of students involved in athletics and other competitive extracurricular activities. Participants may have to submit to random drug testing. This is legal because extracurricular activities are considered a privilege, not a right. Participants may be held to certain standards, such as a minimum GPA and adherence to a code of conduct that forbids the use of drugs. Generally, though, members of the larger student body are tested for drugs only if there is reasonable cause, such as erratic behavior. This is because a high school education is considered a basic right, not a privilege.

Employers may also require drug tests. Laws related to workplace drug testing vary greatly from one state to another. Some cities also have their own statutes. Drug testing may be required before beginning employment, at random, or based on reasonable suspicion, especially if a workplace accident has occurred. An employee may have to sign a consent form before the test, and a teenage employee's parents may be required to give consent.

Parents can legally demand that their children under the age of eighteen submit to a drug test. The American Academy of Pediatrics, however, opposes involuntary drug tests of teenagers.

Drug testing, including random drug testing, is often routine when a sentence of probation is given. One common condition of probation, in fact, is that the individual not test positive for any drug use.

CONSEQUENCES OF A POSITIVE DRUG TEST

Drug testing is intended both as a deterrent and a means of ensuring a safe environment. High school students may be less likely to use drugs if a positive drug test means that they could be excluded from athletics or other activities. A company may enact a drug testing policy in order to guarantee a safe and productive workplace.

A student who fails a drug test faces consequences— for example, an athlete testing positive for drugs is likely to face a penalty, such as suspension from the team. The National Institute on Drug Abuse (NIDA) recommends that schools implement prevention, intervention, and treatment programs in conjunction with drug testing. The organization believes that students with a positive drug test might benefit more from getting help for a drug problem than punishment for a crime. Intervention during high school can help prevent a serious drug problem later in life.

Many schools, however, consider being under the influence of drugs at school to be grounds for suspension or expulsion. If a student fails a drug test administered due to reasonable suspicion, it could lead to disciplinary action—even if the student wasn't actually under the influence of drugs during school hours. Depending on state laws and school policy, it can even lead to criminal charges. Schools have protocols for how to handle such situations— it can be at the school's discretion whether to involve the authorities—but in certain circumstances, in particular at public institutions, school officials may be required to report illegal activity.

Failing a drug test at work may lead to an employee being fired or disciplined. Refusing to take a drug test is generally interpreted as an admission of guilt and may lead to the same consequences as a positive result. If the employer has a zero tolerance policy, an employee will probably be fired and may also be denied unemployment benefits by the state. Some companies, however, will give an employee a second chance if he or she seeks drug treatment. Generally, there are no legal consequences for a positive drug test—a worker may lose the job, but he or she likely won't be arrested.

WHEN YOU HAVE TO GET TREATMENT

Substance abuse can cause an adolescent's life to spin out of control, and drug use tends to be linked with criminal activity. Drug abusers may sell drugs, they may steal in order to buy drugs, or they may commit crimes while under the influence of drugs. A high proportion of teens who are arrested have substance abuse problems. NIDA recommends that all teens detained for any crime be screened for drug abuse.

Drug treatment programs not only help offenders quit using drugs, but they also reduce the chances that offenders will return to a life of crime. Such programs benefit communities and public health as well. But only a small number of offenders are offered effective drug abuse treatment.

Court-mandated drug treatment programs begin with an assessment to determine whether a teen offender will benefit from treatment and what other help might be necessary. Drug abuse may occur along with other issues such as medical problems, mental health issues, physical or emotional abuse, or trouble in school. Often, family involvement helps a young drug abuser through

A student who has tested positive for drug use may receive counseling and other appropriate treatment but may also be subject to disciplinary measures.

the recovery process. When family dynamics are part of the underlying problem, counseling may strengthen family functioning.

A drug treatment program will likely involve the court system, drug abuse treatment providers, social service agencies, and parole or probation supervision. An offender will be monitored through drug testing during the course of the program and during probation, if required. Relapses are not uncommon, and the treatment process incorporates both rewards and punishments in motivating good behavior.

Some communities deal with young drug abusers in a juvenile drug court that specializes in rehabilitating youth offenders. A drug court judge is much more intensively involved in the offender's progress than in regular juvenile court, and the treatment process is more of a collaborative effort between the offender, family, and drug court team than regular court proceedings. These same drug courts also exist in the adult court system. In some circumstances there are mental health courts, which will take on such cases in the absence of a formal drug court, but these do not exist in every system. However, their efficacy has been reported widely, and they are therefore becoming more common.

WHEN YOU WANT TO GET TREATMENT

Sometimes, an adolescent doesn't need to go before a judge in court in order to realize that he or she needs help with a substance abuse problem. Whatever the impetus—trouble in school, a scary experience with drugs, the urging of friends—the next step is to find substance abuse

For some nonviolent young offenders, a drug court program focusing on treatment may provide an effective alternative to ordinary juvenile justice court proceedings.

treatment resources. For many teens, confidentiality may also be a concern.

Federal law offers some privacy and confidentiality for teens receiving substance abuse treatment at federally funded programs and facilities. These might include hospital-based programs, private practices, or nonprofit organizations. A teen must give written consent before a treatment provider can legally disclose information to a parent. In extraordinary circumstances—if the teen poses a threat to his or her own well-being or to another

STEROIDS

Teens tend to become self-conscious about their bodies as they enter adolescence. Boys have generally been subjected to less pressure than girls to conform to unrealistic body types, but the extremely muscular builds depicted in today's action movies and video games may be changing the situation. Teenage boys are becoming increasingly interested in bulking up, and they sometimes turn to anabolic steroids as a shortcut. According to a 2011 CDC survey, among high school students, 4.9 percent of males and 2.4 percent of females had used steroids illicitly.

Anabolic steroids are Schedule III drugs—they are available as a prescription for some medical conditions. They are not intended for use by healthy young adults, and it is illegal to possess steroids without a prescription. Illicitly obtained steroids may have been diverted from legitimate prescriptions, or they may have been manufactured and sold on the black market. It's impossible to know the dosage and quality of these drugs. Federal law allows a maximum penalty of a year in prison and a minimum of a $1,000 fine for possession of steroids. Some states also have their own laws concerning steroids.

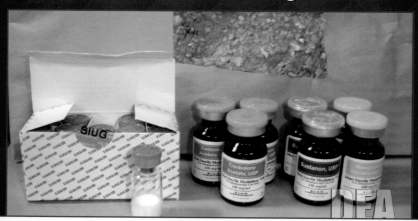

Containers of illicit steroids were seized during a Drug Enforcement Agency (DEA) operation that involved nine countries and raids of dozens of illegal labs in the United States.

person's and lacks the capacity to consent to disclosure— parents may be contacted.

Most state laws do not protect teen confidentiality concerning substance abuse treatment as strictly as federal law. States generally allow minor consent, but with certain limitations. They may impose a minimum age for consent. Many do require parental involvement at some stage of treatment or allow doctors to notify parents without the teen's consent. Some states specifically bar teens from consenting to treatments such as methadone, which is used by recovering heroin addicts.

In some cases, federal and state law may conflict. The subtleties of the law are very complex, and even treatment providers aren't always certain of which law applies in some circumstances. If confidentiality is a serious concern, a teen should ask the treatment provider about consent and privacy rights while reviewing treatment options.

CHAPTER 5

STAYING HEALTHY AT HOME, SCHOOL, AND WORK

Considerations about your health go beyond the door to the doctor's office. You make decisions that affect your health every day concerning matters such as diet, physical activity, and risky behaviors. Some of the factors that influence your health, however, are beyond your control. You might have respiratory problems due to a poorly ventilated apartment. You might become depressed or anxious over harassment at school or work. You might worry about whether a disability or medical condition will make it hard to find a job.

Numerous federal laws exist that guarantee certain rights in matters that involve your health. Landlords are required to meet certain health and safety codes in rental units. Schools need to provide a safe and healthy learning environment. Employers are prohibited from discriminating on the basis of a disability. If your health is affected by conditions at your home, school, or work, there may be recourses and resources available to you.

MEDICAL DISCRIMINATION

Federal law has long prohibited job discrimination based on race, color, religion, sex, or national origin. Employers

Potential employers are prohibited by law from asking job applicants about their medical information or requiring a medical exam as a condition for being hired.

cannot hire or fire anyone based on any of these factors, nor can they treat such employees differently on the job. These rights have been extended to include discrimination based on disability and age.

The law concerning discrimination based on medical conditions is more ambiguous. For someone to qualify as disabled, his or her condition must substantially limit one or more major life activities. Many people dealing with medical conditions are not considered disabled and do not qualify for protection under the law, even if their medical issues affect performance at work or school. The Americans with Disabilities Act does prohibit potential employers from asking about disabilities or requiring medical exams. The Family and Medical Leave Act requires that employees be granted twelve weeks of unpaid leave if they are dealing with a serious medical condition. By law, an employee cannot be fired or demoted, or lose certain other benefits, upon their return from leave.

The Genetic Information Nondiscrimination Act of 2008 added a new category of protection against discrimination. Some people are genetically predisposed to certain medical conditions. This can be determined by genetic testing or predicted by family medical history. It is illegal for employers to discriminate against employees based on genetic information. They are also prohibited from asking about or acquiring genetic information about an employee. In addition, if they do obtain genetic information legally, such as when the employee provided the information voluntarily, they must keep it confidential.

ADDRESSING ABUSE AND HARASSMENT

Whether you're at home, at school, or at work, you have the right to be treated with respect by the people around you. When someone is subjected to cruel or violent treatment, it is called abuse. Abuse goes beyond physical harm—it can also be psychological or emotional. Every type of abuse can have psychological consequences for the victim.

RIGHTS OF THE DISABLED

A number of different federal laws ensure equal opportunities for the disabled. The Americans with Disabilities Act, passed in 1990, prohibits discrimination against people with disabilities in employment, transportation, accessing places open to the public, and other areas of daily life. An employer cannot take an individual's disability into account when hiring, firing, or promoting employees. New public buildings such as schools must be accessible to people in wheelchairs. Telecommunications providers are required to provide services to individuals with speech or hearing disabilities.

Disabled students are granted certain educational rights by the Individuals with Disabilities Education Act, enacted in

The Americans with Disabilities Act specifies certain design standards, such as installing wheelchair accessible ramps, for places of public accommodation, commercial facilities, and state and local government facilities.

1975 and subsequently amended many times. It requires that students with disabilities receive a free, appropriate public education. School staff and parents must develop an Individualized Education Program (IEP) that places a disabled student in the least restrictive environment possible, which may involve time spent both in regular classrooms and in special education courses. Schools are also required to provide certain services to disabled students, such as physical therapy and counseling.

49

Abuse may be physical—such as striking or hitting—and result in injury or pain. Psychological or emotional abuse occurs when the abuser uses words and actions to intimidate, humiliate, or demean the victim. This type of abuse may involve yelling or bullying, but it can also take the form of exclusion or manipulation. It can cause emotional damage just as physical abuse causes physical pain.

Another form of abuse is sexual abuse, which involves touching or other intimate contact without the victim's consent. Minors under a certain age are not legally considered capable of granting sexual consent. The age of consent varies from one state to another, ranging from sixteen to eighteen. An adult over eighteen can be charged with statutory rape, or having sex with an underage minor, even if the underage partner consents. Persons under the age of eighteen may also be charged with statutory rape or sexual assault if the other person involved is significantly younger than them. Specific laws concerning statutory rape vary from one state to another.

When the victim is a minor, any type of abuse qualifies as child abuse. Often, the parents or caregivers are the abusers. In many states, the law allows some physical discipline, such as spanking, but excessive punishment, such as a beating that leaves bruises, is considered abuse. The law is often unclear on the line between physical punishment and abuse. A state law may allow "reasonable" physical discipline, for example, without specifying which actions qualify as "reasonable." Many states still allow corporal punishments in schools.

Neglect of a child is also considered a form of abuse. Parents are expected to provide basic needs, such as adequate food, shelter, hygiene, medical attention, and

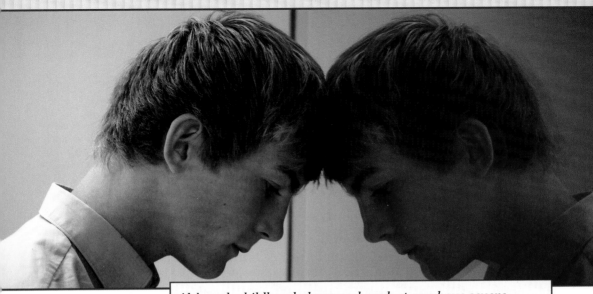

Although childhood abuse and neglect can have severe psychological and physical consequences, treatment measures can help teens overcome the effects of early trauma.

supervision. A child can suffer from emotional neglect by a parent as well as physical neglect. In some states, abandonment qualifies as neglect.

The psychological effects of abuse and neglect can continue long after any physical injuries heal. Children and adolescents who have been abused may suffer from depression. They may have trouble trusting others or suffer from low self-esteem. Sometimes, children who have been abused go on to be abusive themselves as adults.

Cases of abuse should be reported to the police, a social service agency, or another authority figure, such as a teacher or a school nurse. There are also telephone hotlines that offer resources to abuse victims. In order to report a case of abuse, however, it must first be recognized. Family and friends sometimes miss the signs, often because they don't want to admit that there's a serious problem. Victims may have trouble acknowledging that they're being abused, as well, especially when the abuser is someone close to them, such as a relative or significant other. Without intervention, the abuser is likely to continue to inflict harm on the victim.

Harassment is repetitive offensive conduct to another, sometimes based on factors such as race, sex, or disability. Behavior can be considered harassment if it creates a hostile environment, whether at work, at school, or in public places. The offender may be an adult or another student. One common form of harassment is sexual harassment, which might involve unwanted advances, comments, or touching. Both men and women can be the victims of sexual harassment, and both men and women can be the offenders. Persistent harassment can leave a victim feeling stressed and anxious, and it can hurt performance at school or work. Victims of harassment should document incidents and report the behavior to a school official or supervisor.

The penalties for harassment, especially sexual harassment, can be harsh. In some cases, it can even qualify as sexual assault, a felony offense. Students who harass fellow students can be disciplined with punishments as severe as expulsion from school. Depending on age, they may also be charged with criminal offenses.

UNSAFE CONDITIONS

You have a right to stay healthy in your physical environment at home, school, and work, as well. Poor conditions in the places you live, attend school, or work can affect performance as well as health.

A minor's parents are expected to provide acceptable housing for their children. Social service agencies can use uninhabitable living conditions as grounds for removing children from a home. Examples include houses that have been used to produce drugs or that are so filthy that they pose a health hazard. Renters also have rights concerning the condition of their apartment units or rented houses. Although specific requirements vary from one state to another, landlords are expected to maintain the building's structural elements, provide access to services such as electricity and heating, and follow laws regarding matters such as trash disposal and exterminating vermin. If the landlord fails to comply, tenants have recourses such as withholding rent payments. Many cities have agencies or organizations that can help inform renters of their legal rights. In addition, it is illegal for landlords to refuse to rent to tenants because they have children—this qualifies as housing discrimination.

Children and adolescents spend more time in school than in any other environment other than their homes. Nonetheless, many students attend schools that have inadequate ventilation, heat, or lighting. Children are particularly vulnerable to the effects of indoor pollutants, such as dampness and mold, and schools may lack funding to properly maintain and upgrade facilities to address environmental deficiencies. If a student or parent believes that the school environment is causing health problems, they should contact the school administrators.

Young workers also have the right to a safe and healthy workplace. The Occupational Safety and Health Administration (OSHA) sets safety and health standards

Unsafe conditions in buildings can be the result of neglect, outdated technology or construction, or even natural disaster, as in the case of this mold-infested elementary school in New Orleans, Louisiana, which was damaged by Hurricane Katrina.

that apply to most employers in the United States. If your working conditions present the threat of injury or illness, you can report it to OSHA. In addition, there are certain legal restrictions for employing minors. Depending on age, young workers may be limited to working certain hours or be prohibited from working certain types of jobs. Some states require that young workers have a work permit. These restrictions are intended to protect youths' health and safety.

GLOSSARY

act A law or statute passed by a legislative body.

confidentiality The ethical principle that a doctor or other health care provider will not disclose information obtained during the course of a patient's medical care.

consent To agree freely to a course of action, such as a medical examination or treatment.

contraception The intentional prevention of pregnancy through the use of condoms, birth control pills, or other methods.

depression A mental illness in which feelings of sadness, loss, anger, or frustration interfere with everyday life for an extended period of time.

disclose To make known or reveal something such as information that had been private.

discrimination Prejudicial treatment of members of a certain group, based on such factors as class, religion, race, gender, or sexual orientation.

emancipated minor A young adult who takes on adult responsibilities and is granted some legal rights of adults before reaching the age of eighteen.

family planning The practice of limiting the number of children in a family and intentionally spacing out the births.

harassment Unwanted and often aggressive physical or verbal behavior that creates a hostile environment for someone or threatens someone's safety.

HIV Human immunodeficiency virus. The virus that causes AIDS (acquired immune deficiency syndrome).

informed consent A patient's formal agreement to a medical procedure after receiving information about and understanding all of the associated risks and benefits.

juvenile A young person at or beneath the age of juvenile court jurisdiction.

notification The act of sharing official information.

offender One who has committed an illegal act.

penalty A punishment imposed for breaking a rule or law.

prenatal Before birth, or during pregnancy.

privacy Freedom from unwanted intrusion in one's personal matters.

probation The act of suspending an offender's sentence and allowing him or her to go free subject to certain conditions.

prohibit To formally forbid or make illegal.

relapse To fall back into a former condition or practice.

social service A government resource that provides aid, advice, facilities, or other assistance in such areas as education, housing, and medical care.

therapy The treatment of a disease, medical condition, or psychological or behavioral issue.

FOR MORE INFORMATION

American Civil Liberties Union (ACLU)
125 Broad Street, 18th Floor
New York, NY 10004
(212) 549-2500
Website: http://www.aclu.org
The ACLU works to protect and defend individual rights and
liberties guaranteed to everyone in the nation by the
Constitution and laws of the United States.

Canadian Centre on Substance Abuse
75 Albert Street, Suite 500
Ottawa, ON K1P 5E7
Canada
(613) 235-4048
Website: http://www.ccsa.ca
The Canadian Centre on Substance Abuse works to
reduce alcohol- and drug-related harm. It also
advises various organizations on substance abuse
and addiction.

Health Canada
161 Goldenrod Driveway
Ottawa, ON K1A 0K9
Canada
(613) 957-2991
Website: http://www.hc-sc.gc.ca
Health Canada is the federal department responsible for help-
ing the people of Canada improve their health.

Office of Juvenile Justice and Delinquency Prevention (OJJDP)
810 Seventh Street NW

Washington, DC 20531
(202) 307–5911
Website: http://www.ojjdp.gov
Part of the U.S. Department of Justice, OJJDP provides national
leadership, coordination, and resources to prevent and
respond to juvenile delinquency and victimization.

Planned Parenthood
434 West 33rd Street
New York, NY 10001
(212) 541-7800
Website: http://www.plannedparenthood.org
Planned Parenthood provides sexual and reproductive
health care, education, and information to women,
men, and teens.

U.S. Equal Employment Opportunity Commission (EEOC)
131 M Street NE
Washington, DC 20507
(202) 663-4900
Website: http://www.eeoc.gov
The EEOC enforces federal laws banning discrimination in
the workplace.

WEBSITES

Because of the changing nature of Internet links, Rosen
Publishing has developed an online list of websites related to
the subject of this book. This site is updated regularly. Please
use this link to access the list:

http://www.rosenlinks.com/KYR/Heal

FOR FURTHER READING

Bellenir, Karen. *Mental Health Information for Teens: Health Tips About Mental Wellness and Mental Illness Including Facts About Mental and Emotional Health, Depression and Other Mood Disorders, Anxiety Disorders, Behavior Disorders, Self-injury, Psychosis, Schizophrenia, and More.* 3rd ed. Detroit, MI: Omnigraphics, 2010.

Haugen, David M., ed. *Juvenile Justice.* Detroit, MI: Greenhaven Press, 2013.

Haugen, David M., ed. *Labor and Employment.* Detroit, MI: Greenhaven Press, 2012.

Haugen, David M., ed. *Sex.* Detroit, MI: Greenhaven Press, 2013.

Jacobs, Thomas A. *What Are My Rights? Q&A about Teens and the Law.* Minneapolis, MN: Free Spirit Publishing, 2011.

Kaufman, Miriam. *Easy for You to Say: Q&As for Teens Living with Chronic Illness or Disability.* Buffalo, NY: Firefly Books, 2012.

Merino, Noel, ed. *Abortion* (Teen Rights and Freedoms). Detroit, MI: Greenhaven Press, 2013.

Merino, Noel, ed. *Privacy.* Detroit, MI: Greenhaven Press, 2012.

Parks, Peggy J. *Teen Depression.* Detroit, MI: Lucent Books, 2013.

Roizen, Michael F. *You, the Owner's Manual for Teens: A Guide to a Healthy Body and Happy Life.* New York: Free Press, 2011.

Sheff, David. *Clean: Overcoming Addiction and Ending America's Greatest Tragedy.* Boston, MA: Houghton Mifflin Harcourt, 2013.

Shooter, Debbie, and William Shooter. *Drugs and Alcohol 101.* Orlando, FL: Off Campus Education and Publishing Inc., 2010.

BIBLIOGRAPHY

"Board of Ed. of Independent School Dist. no. 92 of Pottawatomie Cty. v. Earls." Legal Information Institute. Retrieved August 20, 2014 (http://www.law.cornell.edu/supct/html/01-332.ZS.html).

Gudeman, Rebecca, and Sara Madge. "The Federal Title X Family Planning Program: Privacy and Access Rules for Adolescents." Youth Law News, January-March 2011. Retrieved August 20, 2014 (http://www.youthlaw.org/publications/yln/2011/jan_mar_2011/the_federal_title_x_family_planning_program_privacy_and_access_rules_for_adolescents).

"Involuntary Commitment And Court-Ordered Treatment." National Alliance on Mental Illness. Retrieved August 24, 2014 (http://www.nami.org/Content/ContentGroups/Policy/Updates/Involuntary_Commitment_And_Court-Ordered_Treatment.htm).

"National Survey Confirms that Youth are Disproportionately Affected by Mental Disorders." National Institute of Mental Health, September 27, 2010. Retrieved September 10, 2014 (http://www.nimh.nih.gov/news/science-news/2010/national-survey-confirms-that-youth-are-disproportionately-affected-by-mental-disorders.shtml).

"Principles of Drug Abuse Treatment for Criminal Justice Populations - A Research-Based Guide." National Institute on Drug Abuse, April 2014. Retrieved August 26, 2014 (http://www.drugabuse.gov/sites/default/files/txcriminaljustice_0.pdf).

"Protecting Minors' Health Information Under The Federal Medical Privacy Regulations." ACLU Reproductive Freedom Project, 2003. Retrieved August 24, 2014

(https://www.aclu.org/files/FilesPDFs/med_privacy
_guide.pdf).

"Reference Card: Minors' Access to Confidential Health Care
in Pennsylvania." American Civil Liberties Union of Pennsylvania, March 2014. Retrieved September 10, 2014
(http://www.aclupa.org/our-work/duvall-reproductive
-freedom-project/minorsaccesstoconfidential/
referencecardminorsaccesst).

Schubert, Carol A., and Edward P. Mulvey. "Behavioral Health
Problems, Treatment, and Outcomes in Serious Youthful
Offenders." Office of Juvenile Justice and Delinquency
Prevention, June 2014. Retrieved September 10, 2014
(http://ojjdp.gov/pubs/242440.pdf).

"Sexual Health of Adolescents and Young Adults in the United
States." Kaiser Family Foundation, Aug 20, 2014.
Retrieved September 10, 2014 (http://kff.org/womens
-health-policy/fact-sheet/sexual-health-of-adolescents
-and-young-adults-in-the-united-states).

"Teen Health Law: Teen health rights information for
California providers of adolescent health services."
National Center for Youth Law. Retrieved August 26,
2014 (http://www.teenhealthlaw.org).

"Understanding Confidentiality and Minor Consent in
California: An Adolescent Provider Toolkit." Adolescent
Health Working Group and California Adolescent Health
Collaborative, February 11, 2011. Retrieved August
15, 2014 (http://www.californiateenhealth.org/wp
-content/uploads/2011/06/toolkit-rri-Web.pdf).

"Vance v. Spencer County Public School District." FindLaw.
Retrieved August 26, 2014 (http://caselaw.findlaw
.com/us-6th-circuit/1179326.html).

INDEX

A

abuse, 17, 48, 50–52
Affordable Care Act (ACA), 25
alcohol, 13, 16, 37
American Academy of Pediatrics (AAP), 19–20, 38
American Medical Association (AMA), 18
Americans with Disabilities Act, 48, 49

C

Centers for Disease Control and Prevention (CDC), 18, 24, 28, 44
confidentiality, 7, 11–15, 16, 18, 22, 30, 43, 45
consent, 6, 7, 8–11, 12, 14–15, 16
  for contraceptives, 22
  for drug testing, 36, 38
  informed, 9
  for mental health treatment, 30, 32–33
  parental, 9, 12–14, 24, 32, 33, 38
  for prenatal care, 24
  sexual, 50
  for STD testing, 26
  for substance abuse treatment, 43, 45
contraceptives/birth control, 20–22, 25
correctional facilities, 35

D

Department of Health and Human Services, 20, 25
depression, 4, 7, 14, 28, 30, 51
disabled, 47, 49
drug testing, 36–40
drug treatment, 40–45

E

eating disorders, 14

F

Family and Medical Leave Act, 48
Family Educational Rights and Privacy Act (FERPA), 16
Food and Drug Administration (FDA), 22

G

Genetic Information Nondiscrimination Act, 48

H

harassment, 4, 6, 46, 48, 52
health care costs, 15, 25
health insurance, 11, 15, 16, 25, 32
Health Insurance Portability and Accountability Act (HIPAA), 16
HIV, 16, 25, 26

ABOUT THE AUTHOR

Jason Porterfield is a writer and journalist who has written many books for Rosen. Several of his previous books have also focused on health and legal issues concerning teens, including *How to Beat Social Alienation* and *Teen Stress and Anxiety.* He lives in Chicago.

ABOUT THE EXPERT REVIEWER

Lindsay A. Lewis, Esq., is a practicing criminal defense attorney in New York City, where she handles a wide range of matters, from those discussed in this series to high-profile federal criminal cases. She believes that each and every defendant deserves a vigorous and informed defense. Ms. Lewis is a graduate of the Benjamin N. Cardozo School of Law and Vassar College.

PHOTO CREDITS

Cover Shutterstock.com/MichaelJay; cover (background), p. 1 Christophe Rolland/Shutterstock.com; pp. 4–5 Rengim Mutevellioglu/Moment/Getty Images; p. 8 slobo/E+/Getty Images; pp. 10–11 Monkey Business Images/Shutterstock.com; pp. 12–13 Camille Tokerud/Iconica/Getty Images; p. 17 Fuse/Getty Images; pp. 18–19 Lucky Business/Shutterstock.com; p. 21 Brendan Smialowski/Getty Images; p. 23 Paul Schlemmer/Shutterstock.com; pp. 26–27 Joseph Abbott/E+/Getty Images; pp. 28–29 Rob Marmion/Shutterstock.com; p. 31 Glow Wellness/Getty Images; pp. 34–35, 54 © AP Images; p. 37 Photostock-Israel/Science Photo Library/Getty Images; pp. 40–41 Pamela Moore/E+/Getty Images; p. 43 Rich Legg/E+/Getty Images; p. 44 DEA/Getty Images; p. 47 Nick White and Fiona Jackson-Downes/Cultura/Getty Images; p. 49 Huntstock/Getty Images; p. 51 Marcel ter Bekke/Moment/Getty Images.

Designer: Brian Garvey; Editor: Shalini Saxena